CRUDE HINTS TOWARDS AN HISTORY OF MY HOUSE

*Portrait of John Soane (1753-1837) by William Owen (1769-1825), oil on canvas, 1805 (SM P228)*

# Crude Hints towards an History of my House in Lincoln's Inn Fields

## by Sir John Soane

## Introduction

### by Helen Dorey

Archaeopress Publishing Ltd
Gordon House
276 Banbury Road
Oxford OX2 7ED
www.archaeopress.com

ISBN 978 1 78491 215 4

Text and images © Sir John Soane's Museum 2015

Cover illustration: The Monument Court at 13 Lincoln's Inn Fields under construction, 31 August to 2 September 1812 (SM Vol.83/5)

All rights reserved. No part of this book may be reproduced, stored in retrieval system, or transmitted, in any form or by any means, electronic, mechanical, photocopying or otherwise, without the prior written permission of the copyright owners.

Printed in England by 4edge, Hockley
This book is available direct from Archaeopress or from our website www.archaeopress.com

# Contents

*Crude Hints:* an Introduction ................................................................... 1

Note on the Manuscript ........................................................................... 17

Transcript of Crude Hints towards a History of my house ................. 19

Notes to the transcript ............................................................................ 33

ii

# *Crude Hints:* an Introduction

*Crude Hints towards an history of my house*, written by Soane in August and September 1812, must surely be one of the strangest and most perplexing documents in the history of English architecture. In it Soane, in the guise of *An Antiquary*, imagines his home as a future ruin inspected by visitors speculating on its origins and function. The manuscript is dated 30 August, 7 Sept and 22 Sept and was written in the year that Soane was rebuilding No. 13 Lincoln's Inn Fields as his residence – his home was at the time a demolition site evolving into a completed building rather than as envisaged in the manuscript a finished structure mouldering into ruin.

The demolition of the existing No. 13 house began on 17th July 1812 after two days when materials of the existing house were auctioned off on the site. The buyers had to clear away their own purchases so in effect they carried out the demolition – creating an evolving ruin in the process. Work then began on the rebuilding of the house – interrupted by rain and time off on 17th August to 'drink the health of Ld Wellington & his brave Army' (on Sunday 16th August Wellington's victory at the Battle of Salamanca was announced). Soane's progress notebook reveals that by the 30th August, the first date on the Crude Hints manuscript, the front brick wall of the house was completed and some floors had been inserted but the house remained a shell. Work was only just beginning on the foundations for the buildings either side of the central courtyard and the first stone of the projecting white Portland stone façade had been laid by the masons on 26th August – only four days before Soane began writing. The front part of the house was therefore a construction site which could be viewed imaginatively as either partly built or partly ruined. Visible behind it were Soane's earlier buildings – his purpose-designed single-storey 'museum' and office running across the back of the No. 13 site – constructed in 1808-9 as an extension to his previous house at No. 12 Lincoln's Inn Fields. No. 12 stood alongside the construction site, next door to the west.

In *Crude Hints* Soane speculates first as to whether the house will be interpreted as a Roman temple (perhaps dedicated to Jupiter), a burial site, a convent or monastery or a magician's lair? He notes that the ruins are supposed by antiquarians to have been enlarged at different times and formed from the ruins of others – this is true to an extent as Soane's buildings in Lincoln's Inn Fields were built over a number of years and on the ruins of those he pulled down to make way for them. The 'clues' to the origins of the building which are presented for the most part relate closely to Soane's existing building and his collections. The ammonite fossils on the rear roofs[1] are interpreted as symbols of 'Jupiter Ammon' and the cast of the famous Roman statue

---

[1] Soane placed ammonite fossils on the skyline of his Office when he raised its roof in 1821. Although we do not know for certain that they were in his collection as early as 1812 this reference makes it highly likely that they were placed on the rear roofs in that year – to be viewed from his newly built house on the front of the site.

of the *Apollo Belvedere* in the Museum seen as perhaps the founder of the building, a magician or necromancer, turned into stone.² The Museum itself is interpreted variously as a chapel or as a place of burial³ whilst the windowless top-lit staircase is seen as a prison, similar to one of Piranesi's nightmare imaginary visions in his *Carceri*.⁴ Two *caryatids* in the courtyard are seen as possible clues to the Greek origin of the building – perhaps *supporting part of the roof of a peristyle*. The tone is deliberately antiquarian with the Monument Court referred to in several places by the Latin *cavaedium* (in various spellings) and the occasional use of archaic words such as *yclept* and *burded*. In the years leading up to the writing of *Crude Hints* Soane had spent a great deal of time studying the 'first origins' of architecture for his Royal Academy lectures and this is reflected in the manuscript, with allusions in passing to Semiramis, Minach, Egypt and Noah's Ark as well as to the Roman world. Soane's vision of his home as a ruin is that of a man imbued with memories of the great ruins of antiquity which he had explored in Italy during his Grand Tour. The basement is envisaged as a series of subterranean crypts and catacombs, entered only through a small aperture from above – thought by some to be a coal hole (a suggestion Soane ridicules in his antiquarian guise – in fact the aperture at the back of the building was for lowering barrels into the cellar from the road behind) whilst the carved blocks resembling the lids of cinerary urns on the rear façade remind him of a place of burial. A reference to the absence of 'burded cypresses' show that Soane had in mind Roman imperial burial sites – an idea which perhaps led on to his speculation that the niches on his rustic rear façade might have contained statues of the twelve Caesars. Fragmentary inscriptions, like those scattered amongst the ruins of Rome, are discovered on the site.

The house as envisaged in *Crude Hints* partially existed only in Soane's imagination. There is speculation about the reason for the presence of the two caryatids on the front façade. Whilst these are shown on the design drawings of July and August 1812 they were not actually delivered to site and installed on the building until October 6th (several weeks after the last date on the manuscript). Soane also seems to elide the building as it was being constructed with an idea for a much more grandiose scheme which was in his mind at the time but not drawn up until January 1813 (Fig. 1). Among the clues to this is the passage referring to a striking example of an open loggia *about the centre of the north front of this place* [Lincoln's Inn Fields] *where an attempt has been made with two old houses to form one united mass of building and to produce this effect a grand portico is introduced similar to those of the ancient temples*. There is also a reference to an external Ionic colonnade which may relate to this design. While Soane is writing a fusion is taking place in

---

² It is interesting to note this early parallel drawn between Apollo and the 'Founder' i.e. Soane himself. Years later, in late 1833 after the passing of the Soane Museum Act of Parliament in April that year, Soane moved a bust of himself by Sir Francis Chantrey from a modest position in the Tivoli Recess off the main staircase down to the Dome Area. There it is placed opposite the *Apollo Belvedere* placing the two in deliberate association once again.
³ Again, this prefigures later developments.
⁴ See note 15 to the *Crude Hints* manuscript.

*Fig. 1 Design for an extended façade for Nos 13-15 Lincoln's Inn Fields, drawn by Joseph Michael Gandy, January 1813 (SM 74/4/1)*

*Fig. 2 John Soane, hypothetical reconstruction of the ruins at Pitzhanger Manor, Ealing, showing the Corinthian portico of a Roman temple on a rusticated podium, facing a precinct formed by two colonnaded wings, 1804 (SM Soane Case 31, ff. 84-85)*

his mind of existing designs for his evolving building with the reality of the construction site, his existing collections and his vision of the future.

*Crude Hints* was not Soane's first essay into the world of ruins. In 1802 he had written a light-hearted account of the mock ruins he had erected at Pitzhanger Manor at Ealing, his country home, speculating upon their origins. In his *Memoirs* he recalled how guests at large parties held at Pitzhanger to coincide with Ealing Fair had enjoyed such speculations and it seems that he employed his pupils to draw the ruins 'reconstructed' in preparation for one such party in 1804 (Fig. 2).

*Crude Hints*, in contrast to the Ealing manuscript, begins in a spirit of light-hearted imaginative speculation but soon descends into something much darker and more personal. The figure of the 'founder' or 'creator' of the ruins under discussion gradually comes to the fore and the text becomes a tortured and bitter lament for the failure of his dynastic ambitions and an account of perceived vendettas against him. The frenetic handwriting indicates an almost manic outpouring written in great agony of mind and, according to the annotations, in just three weeks.

At the time the manuscript was written Soane had been coming slowly and painfully to the realisation that his two sons – John and George – were not going to follow him into the architectural profession, nor found an architectural dynasty (Fig. 3). John had recently gone through a fairly disastrous period of architectural training in Liverpool with Joseph Gandy and had ongoing health problems. He had also recently contracted a marriage which whilst acceptable was not especially welcomed by his parents. George, Soane's younger son, was continuously pestering his parents for money and attempting to make a living as a novelist and playwright. Soane had put Pitzhanger Manor on the market in 1807 (it was finally sold in 1810) partly as a result of his sons' indifference and this disappointment is expressed strongly in *Crude Hints* in the section in which the antiquary speculates on the meaning of a fragmentary inscription '*et filii filiorum*' discovered amongst the ruins. The author rails against *the vanity of human expectations* lamenting that *the man who founded this place fondly imagined that the children of his children would have inhabited the place for ages – Oh! what a falling off do these ruins present*. The inscription – with its biblical tone (it is used in two passages in the Old Testament referring to successive generations dwelling in a particular land) – is seen as a melancholy epitaph for Soane himself.

In 1806 Soane had been appointed Professor of Architecture at the Royal Academy and it is his relations with the Royal Academy which provide a clue to a major underlying reason for the sense of vendetta apparent in *Crude Hints*. On his appointment Soane commenced a long period of intensive study in preparation for the lectures he would be expected to give each year. He commenced his first full series of six lectures in January 1810. The lectures proceeded smoothly until the fourth lecture on 29th January 1810, in which Soane criticised a number of recent buildings including George Dance's Royal College of Surgeons (begun 1806 but not completed until 1813; Fig. 4) and the Covent Garden Theatre (now the Royal Opera House; Fig. 5) – completed in 1809

*Fig. 3 George Soane (left) and John Soane junior, the sons of John Soane, by William Owen, 1805 (SM P229)*

*Fig. 4 Design perspective of the façade of the Royal College of Surgeons, drawn to show the effect of the proposed portico, George Dance the younger, 1808 (SM Dance 3/13/9)*

*Fig. 5 Royal Academy Lecture drawing of Robert Smirke's Covent Garden Theatre, dated 20 Dec. 1809, one of several of the building that Soane so disastrously criticised in January 1810 (SM 18/9/2)*

to the designs of Robert Smirke (1780-1867). He criticised the buildings for their *utter want of appropriate character* and their combination of meanness and pretension – especially in having grandiose front façades combined with mean side elevations – sacrificing everything to one front of the building. Soane was careful, however, not to name the architects concerned and to point out that these defects could have been the result of financial pressures. Soane's comments were greeted with hissing from the audience and Smirke's associates – especially his father, Robert Smirke, and the diarist Joseph Farington – immediately launched a campaign against him within the Council of the Academy, bringing forward a motion to prevent lecturers criticising the work of living artists.

As a result of the passing of this motion (Soane's was the only vote against it!) Soane suspended his lectures in the midst of the course. He then refused to budge from this position despite an attempt in 1811 to have him replaced as Professor on the grounds that he was not lecturing. He relented sufficiently to give two lectures in January 1812 but then announced that he would not do so again until the motion was rescinded. The situation was still at this impasse in late 1812 and Soane's mounting sense of unjust persecution at the hands of the Royal Academy Council must have been at the forefront of his mind during the period when he was writing *Crude Hints*. It helps to explain what some contemporaries referred to as his paranoid and intemperate behaviour between 1810 and 1813 which is reflected in the long section of the manuscript which relates to the dispute. This passage demonstrates clearly how close to the truth J.C. Rossi the sculptor was when he described Soane's behaviour at a Royal Academy Council meeting in April 1811 as 'that of an insane man' as it gradually changes from a restrained argument into a wild outpouring of resentment:

> *He never gave himself a moment's time to reflect on who was the author of the work he criticised..... He went on from a pure love to promote the interests of Art, until at last he had raised a nest of wasps about him sufficient to sting the strongest man to death – Revenge <u>levelled</u> tales of dishonour at him, which no innocence of heart or integrity of conduct could set right and to wind up the tragedy cruelty and cowardice, twin ruffians set on by malice in the dark combined together to strike at his infirmities and mistakes:– then persecutions and other misfortunes of a more direct & domestic nature preyed on his mind – he saw the views of early youth blighted – his fairest prospects utterly destroyed – his lively character became sombre – melancholy, brooding constantly over an accumulation of evils brought him into a state little short of mental derangement, his enemies perceived this – they seized the moment – they smote his rock & he fell as many had done before him and died as was generally believed of <u>a broken heart</u>.*

Soane may also have his own ostracism and near mental collapse in mind when he speculates that a windowless void (the staircase) might have been a punishment block where victims were left alone to starve to death in all the horror of endless darkness, there to pay the forfeit of a little human frailty, adding here is food for meditation even to madness.

Whereas in *Crude Hints* the founder of the house is said to have died of a broken heart Soane himself was campaigning vigorously in his dispute with the Academy at the time when *Crude Hints* was written. He was working on a substantial pamphlet about the lecture dispute, *An Appeal to the Public occasioned by the Suspension of the Architectural Lectures in the Royal Academy...* vindicating his position, summarising the history of his persecution by the Academy and expressing further criticisms of the Covent Garden Theatre and the Royal College of Surgeons. Soane distributed copies of his pamphlet to friends but at their recommendation it was not published widely. It is interesting in this context that there are indications in *Crude Hints* that as he was writing Soane was thinking about the possible publication of the manuscript.

In fact right was somewhat on Soane's side in the lecture dispute – he expressed his criticisms discreetly and there does seem to have been a conspiracy against him at the Academy, so his sense of persecution was perhaps not misplaced.

The last straw for Soane in 1812 was that he was pursued by the District Surveyor over the façade to his new house in Lincoln's Inn Fields and this impending litigation, initiated but unresolved at the dates when the manuscript was written, seems to have provided the immediate spur for the writing of *Crude Hints*.

Early on in the manuscript Soane refers to the fact that *much offence was taken by many to the composition* of the façade of the building, adding *attempts were made … to render the whole abortive* by *an officer yclept a District Surveyor.* This is a reference to William Kinnard, District Surveyor for the parishes of St Giles-in-the Fields and St George, Bloomsbury since 1807 and in 1812 still only twenty-four. Kinnard was said by a contemporary to have been a man who *went mad from time to time* and if he did so with Soane it must have been an unfortunate conjunction.[5]

The façade dispute revolved around the design of the projecting Portland stone 'virandah' or 'loggia', open on three floors, which Soane proposed to add to the front of No. 13 Lincoln's Inn Fields. The front of the house is shown in Fig. 6 (of *c.* August 1812) almost as executed with the projecting loggia on three floors, the upper section flanked by balconies on the parapets of which are two female caryatids based on those of the Erechtheion in Athens.

The District Surveyor objected to this three-storey projection on the grounds that it contravened the Building Act. Since the early 17th century various Acts had been passed outlawing projections and seeking to enforce uniform street façades – hence the Georgian terrace. The Building Act in force in 1812 was that passed in 1774 which specified that frames should be set in reveals and excluded woodwork, with few exceptions, from façades. It stipulated that *no Box-window or*

---

[5] J.L. Woolf as quoted in Howard Colvin, *Dictionary of British Architects*, entry for Kinnard/Kinnaird.

*Fig. 6 Design perspective of the façade of 13 Lincoln's Inn Fields, drawn by Joseph Michael Gandy c. August 1812 (SM 14/6/2 Photograph Ole Woldbye)*

*other projection shall .... extend beyond the general Line of the fronts of the houses* unless for *open Porticoes, steps or iron Pallisades* [railings].

It is not known how Kinnard heard about Soane's façade before it was built but Soane's Diary notes that on 12th August (at a date when the building of the loggia had not begun) *Kinnard called and behaved impudently*.[6] No doubt Soane responded forthrightly and the surveyor then retaliated by bringing a court action on the grounds that Soane had contravened the Building Act. Soane was writing *Crude Hints* on 30th August & 7th and 22nd September and it was on the 8th September that Kinnard sent Soane formal *notice of the building being against the regulations of the Building Act* adding that he would lay a complaint before the magistrates and it was in the context of this pending court case that Soane was writing during September. On the date that the initial notice arrived the construction of the ground-floor level of the projecting loggia was completed and Soane could record that *the Carpenters began setting the horses for the first landing in front*.[7]

In fact it was not until 26th September that a summons arrived for the 28th. In the interim Thomas Leverton, a friend of Soane, surveyed the house and found nothing wrong with the façade. He seems to have pleaded with Soane to allow him to intercede with Kinnard in advance of the court hearing but Soane would not allow him to do so saying that he *wished the Kinnards to proceed to the Quarter Sessions – or do what they pleased*. The case came to court on 28th September but was postponed and again postponed on 7th October. It was eventually heard on the 12th October and *The Sun* newspaper of 15th October 1812 reported that during the case Soane's lawyer had *stated that so far from Mr. Soane's building (of which he exhibited a model) being an injury, it was an ornament to the Square, and he produced models of two other buildings, namely Mr. Pearce's and Surgeon's Hall, of far greater projection, the one which had received the sanction of the Magistrates upon a similar information having been laid and the other had never been complained of at all.* Judgement was given against Kinnard and Soane was able to complete his façade to his intended design. Despite the fact that the Building Act prohibiting projections was still in force Soane did eventually progressively enclose the loggia in the 1820s and 30s, incorporating it into the rooms behind on each level.

*Crude Hints* reveals much about Soane's attitude to the façade, deducing that it *must have been raised by some fanciful mind smitten with the love of novelty in direct defiance of all the established rules of the architectural schools*. Soane was very critical of private houses for their lack of 'expressed character' on façades, singling out in his lectures the uniform dreary façades erected by speculative builders and in draft sections on portals and balconies (not used in the final lectures) was even critical of his own balcony at No. 12 Lincoln's Inn Fields for being without visible means of support.

---

[6] SNB 12 August 1812 (Soane Archive).
[7] Soane Archive Notebook 7/A/8, a diary kept by Soane recording the progress of the construction of No.13 in Summer 1812.

He praised 'character' as expressed, for example, in the oriel window at Grocers' Hall which gave the façade a variety of contrasts of light and angle. All these ideas were in his mind as he began his façade design for No. 13. He was also thinking of the general effect on the north side of Lincoln's Inn Fields where the houses were of irregular design but all with a common building line and all in brick. Soane had stayed within the regulations of the Building Act when he constructed the façade of No. 12 Lincoln's Inn Fields in 1792-4 although it did have novel features, being constructed in white Norfolk bricks (which would have stood out like stone amongst the other brick houses) with a brick cornice at the top – a rustic feature he had used in outbuildings for country houses, at the stables at Chelsea Hospital and on the rear façade of No. 13 (on the site of former stables) – and having an elongated S-shape normally associated with neo-classical tombs for the balcony railing. Although a modest façade, No. 12 was Soane's own personal version of a standard house front. At No. 13 Soane put into practice his idea that style should express character in harmony with the interior. His projecting façade singled out the house as a building of importance, much as a portico would have done and evoked an Italianate loggia overlooking a square. In *Crude Hints* Soane comments that the *aspect of this front being to the South the kind of awning or verandah storey is not misapplied...... particularly as it does not seem to have darkened any of the apartments.*

Soane's own final conclusion about the façade as expressed in this manuscript is that its construction was justified by the search for beauty and picturesque effects. These ideas were amplified in an article in the *European Magazine* of November 1812. The writer had obviously been briefed by Soane himself and stated that the façade was designed to render No. 13 more conspicuous than No. 12 conferring on it *a consequence commensurate to its scientific purpose...& the collection it contains....* The author acknowledges that the façade does *break the line....but in a manner so elegant that it is an advantage* and goes on to assert that a terrace cannot be picturesque in its long monotony. This justification in terms of the picturesque is then related to Soane's large Canaletto painting of the *Riva degli Schiavoni* in which any possible dull uniformity is broken up with *variety of every kind* (Fig. 7). The façade, if viewed with the eye of a painter, relieves the eye when drawn along the terrace on the north side of Lincoln's Inn Fields, acting as an 'eye catcher'.

Soane uses the opportunity of discussion of the façade to reiterate his criticisms of George Dance's Royal College of Surgeons opposite. He points out that his own caryatids are opposite two statues on top of the Royal College of Surgeons on the south side of the Fields and alleges that the District Surveyor has been *taught to believe* that the caryatids were placed here deliberately to *ridicule* the statues opposite *where two old men with Greek names on their skirts are represented embracing a sort of shield.* He goes on to speculate that these figures (which actually represent Machaon and Podalirius) may represent two famous misers who once had a pawnbroking business on the site. This is an allusion to Soane's criticism of the building for its combination of *extravagance and parsimony.* In the later *Descriptions* of his residence Soane again mentions the two statues on the Royal College of Surgeons as being opposite his own caryatids and he obviously

*Fig. 7 Canaletto, Riva degli Schiavoni looking west, Sir John Soane's Museum (SM P66)*

wanted readers to contrast the two set of figures – to the benefit of his own. He seems to have intended an element of intentional ridicule of the Royal College of Surgeons despite the personal debt he owed to its architect George Dance, his first architectural master.[8]

*Crude Hints* allows Soane to present his own motives for the setting up of his museum as part of the speculation. The Antiquary relates that some have supposed the origin of the *strange and mixed assemblage* of casts and fragments in the Museum *might have been for the advancement of Architectural knowledge* among students *who had no means of visiting Greece and Italy*, giving them *better ideas of ancient Works than would be conveyed through the medium of drawings or prints.* The visitor is urged to imagine the ruin *as the dwelling of an artist, architect or painter. If an architect*, he continues, *thus we throw new light on the subject* and *account most satisfactorily for that great assemblage of ancient fragments in the interior of the building which must have been placed there for the advancement and knowledge of ancient art.* This represents a summary of Soane's own first thoughts about establishing an Academy of Art. He wrote elsewhere that *On my appointment to the Professorship I began to arrange the Books, casts and models in order that the students might have the benefit of easy access to them*[9] and at his lecture on 6th January 1812 he had announced publicly to his Royal Academy students that they could visit his house the day before and the day after his lectures to inspect his collection. The *European Magazine* picked up this intention in November 1812 when it referred to the house as an 'Academy' of Architecture, although since Soane's lectures did not resume until 12 February 1813 presumably no students visited the house in the interim period.

The reasons for Soane's public announcement in 1812 that he was opening up his house to students were probably complex. He may have wanted to show how liberal he was and, bearing in mind the lecture dispute, he may at that moment have wished to promote his house as a rival resource for Royal Academy students – thus bolstering his own position. His sons were not interested and so he needed to find a purpose for his rapidly growing collection and he had a genuine wish to benefit architectural education. He believed that young architects unable to take a Grand Tour needed to see objects in three dimensions, through the medium of casts and fragments, as well as prints and drawings and he was also only too aware that the resources of the Royal Academy were inadequate – because of this he had himself as a student in the 1770s used William Chambers' personal library for study.

---

[8] Soane's son John wrote to his father about the new elegant façade of No. 13, clearly referring to the College of Surgeons opposite, 'will not the patch-work on the opposite side frown? … let it do so, the very thought does me good'. Gillian Darley (*John Soane: An Accidental Romantic*, p.211) quotes this letter and explains that Soane had wished to be considered for the commission to build the Royal College of Surgeons and found his omission galling.

[9] See Gillian Darley, *John Soane: An Accidental Romantic,* for details of Soane's bad relationship with Dance and their eventual rapprochement.

Soane's house was a visual version of his Royal Academy lectures and although *Crude Hints* represents a melancholy vision of it as a mouldering ruin, engendered by his sense of persecution, it does encapsulate his vision for the future of his museum as an 'Academy of Architecture'.

*Detail of Fig. 14*

# Note on the Manuscript

The *Crude Hints* manuscript (SM Soane Case 31) is inscribed on the title page *Crude Hints towards an history of my house in L.I.F.* The first page of the text is headed *Crude Hints / 30 Aug: 1812 / 7 Sepr. / 22d Septr.* Most of the pages are numbered in Soane's hand either in pen or pencil. The sheets include three which appear to represent variant endings to the text: one of these is inscribed as such by Soane.

> *The manuscript is written on sheets of laid paper with a variety of different watermarks and countermarks as follows:*
> *Title page, pp. 1, 7, 19, 31, 33, 43, 45, 55, 59 and unnumbered sheet p. 63 (a variant ending mentioning drawings of 1830): watermark: Britannia in a crowned oval*
> *Blank unnumbered sheet between title page & p.1: watermark: J Larkin [trimmed] / 1812*
> *pp.3, 9, 11, 17, 39, 41, 47, 51: watermark: DUSAUTOY & RUMP / 1808*
> *p.5, 15, 21, 23, 25, 27, 29, 37: watermark: GOLDING / & / SNELGROVE / 1807*
> *p.13 and the page numbered 55 but placed as p.61 in the sequence: watermark: Britannia in crowned oval with monogram GJ beneath*
> *p.35: watermark: J WHATMAN / 1810*
> *pp.53 & 57: watermark: J ANSELL / 1810*

The paper and watermarks seem to show that the manuscript was written using a variety of papers available in Soane's office and there are no pages that appear to have been added later. This is particularly important in relation to the three variant endings to the text.

As is often the case with drafts prepared by Soane, the text of *Crude Hints* is written in a single column down the right-hand side of the page, leaving ample space for marginal notes which are written in two further columns to the left (see Fig. 8). In editing the text Soane's extensive and often illegible deletions have been omitted. In a number of places alternative words or phrases are written in above the text: these are shown in square brackets. In places the preferred phrase or word is underlined and this is also shown. On a small number of occasions an alternative choice of word is written in the margin alongside the main text column and prefixed by *v.* for 'versus'. Suggested transliterations by Arthur Bolton (Curator 1917-45) are written in pencil above or below many words – some of these are incorrect.

*Crude Hints* is bound with another manuscript, an account of the ruins at Pitzhanger Manor, Soane's country house in Ealing, headed *Ealing / June 1802*, in a different hand and written on paper watermarked *C PATCH / 1801*. This is followed by a number of watercolour sketches of the Pitzhanger ruins restored as architectural compositions (see Fig. 2). These were clearly once secured to the Pitzhanger manuscript by the upper left-hand corners with thread. A further sheet of manuscript is also bound with *Crude Hints* which seems to be a rough draft of a preface to Soane's Royal Academy lectures. These manuscripts have no direct connection with *Crude Hints* and were not bound with it originally. The bookplate is inscribed by Arthur Bolton (Curator 1917-45), *MSS Bound for Curator's use / Arthur T. Bolton FSA / July 23 1919*.

I would like to thank Professor Robin Middleton of Columbia University and Susan Palmer, Archivist at Sir John Soane's Museum, for their help with the transcription of the manuscript and Susan Palmer for her assistance with some of the footnotes.

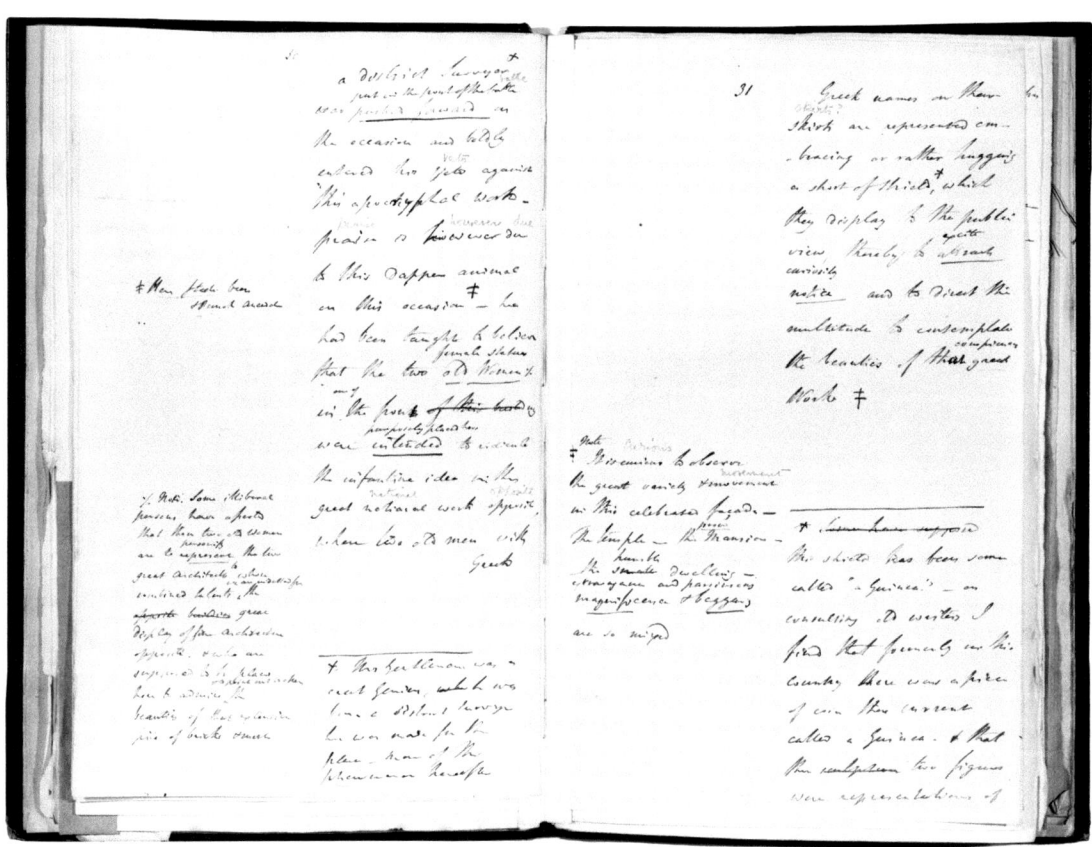

*Fig. 8 Pages from the Crude Hints MS (ff.30-31)*

Crude Hints towards an History of my House in L[incoln's] I[nn] Fields[1]

Crude Hints
30 Aug: 1812
7 Sepr.
22d Sept.

In this age of research when the Connoisseur and the Antiquary find a lively interest in whatever relates to former times & their attention is thereby frequently directed to the investigation of things which, at least to common minds, seem of little importance, no wonder, in such an age, so much notice has been taken of the ruins and very extensive assemblage of fragments of ancient works partly buried and in some degree attached to a building in this metropolis apparently of later date [2] [in Lincoln's Inn Fields (del.)] – to rescue this work from its present uncertain origin and that the public should be fully [better] informed respecting these ruins and be led to have an interest in them, I shall collect together the various conjectures which have been made respecting this building and also the data on which these speculative opinions have been raised. I shall likewise point out the improbability of some of those hypotheses and also my own opinions on the subject, hoping thereby to call the attention of others better <u>qualified</u> [gifted] than myself to rescue this plan from its present unmarked uncertainty &c.

This building has been supposed <u>to have been</u> of much greater extent than appears from the remains now to be seen – & it is also presumed to have been enlarged at different times [3] and, its decorations suggest, and [sic] in some degree formed from the ruins of others of a more magnificent and interesting <u>description</u> [4] – but we are so completely in the dark on the subject of this structure, that to ascertain with any hope of precision either the periods in which it was founded – its extent, or on what occasions or for what purposes it was originally destined will be found to be no moderate task & such as will require no small portion of penetration and reflexion [sic]:- for this undertaken [sic] we have but <u>few data</u>, except the scanty materials

    v. character

which the present remains of this building offer together with some few traditionary [sic] memorials.

From the style of some parts of the Architecture this work has been supposed anterior to the time of Augustus* [and apparently (del.)] long before Architecture had attained that high polish which the works of the Augustan Age so clearly possessed – other reasons equally plausible have been adduced [from the same sources (del.)]* to establish a contrary opinion*.

There are no Staircase [sic] in the present remains, proof of the structure having been more extensive.

v. and perhaps

* Note. I say apparently for it is possible Architecture might have been better understood at that period in Italy than in Britain – in the succeeding times the Britons were designated "barbaros Brittannos".
*i.e. The component parts of the building now remaining.
*A Votive foot & hand indicate this building to have been a temple[5] – and the *cornu ammonis* designate it as dedicated to Jupiter.[7] The Columns describe a Colonnade of a kind almost peculiar to Convents, and as these Cols: [sic] are of the Ionic or Feminine order it is reasonable to conclude from thence that it had been a convent of Nuns, & not a Heathen Temple.[8] The Sphinx, The Griffon & Lamb carry us very far back into Antiquity[9] – & the flat vaulted Ceiling of the great Crypt is in itself so truly Egyptian that [10]

[UNFINISHED NOTE]

See Customs of the Ancients[6]

Sphinx – Egyptian Griffon

I am at a loss to reconcile this idea to the real fact [sic] of the case, for it is well known that foundations of brick & stone, or in other words of the same kind of materials as those to be found in various parts of the substructions of this very building:– I am aware such reasoning would make our work very extensive indeed*
but what of that – read the accounts of ancient works which we know from their present remains were spread over many acres*

* Certainly – Is not all London built of the same trash nearly – some people can swallow anything. here quote in a note some extended accounts from Arabian Tales, Roman etc.
*The streets of Nineveh[11] were three days in extent & Noahs Ark[12] contained accommodation for I tremble to say what.

We fancy we hear him repeat with enthusiastic satisfaction the words "mihi turpe(?)

relinqui est" recollecting how often he had used this in Rome when deliberating between going and staying*[13]

\* Note. Surely it is not too much to suppose his mind so forcibly struck with these words that he instantly composed an Ode to Augustus on the occasion and altho' we have only this fragment of it remaining, and that misplaced, yet the thing was possible.

Thus much for one of the inscriptions, the other will be hereafter noticed:– it is to be observed that notwithstanding this building consisted of several stages or stories (like some of the buildings of Semiramis)[14] no vestiges remain of a staircase of any kind – hence it is fair to conclude that the extent of the building was greater than its present remains shew – for a Staircase there must have been\*

\* Note. Admitted – but at the same time there is a space, well suited for a Staircase as it would communicate most easily with the different rooms now existing in the building – I am aware it has been supposed that this very space, if a staircase, could only have been one of those Carcerian dark Staircases represented in some of Piranesi's ingenious dreams for prisons[15]: – those who argue thus forget that a staircase may be [might have been] lighted by a Skylight – & it must be recollected that this reasoning at least makes in favour of the great Antiquity of this Design which some have doubted – skylights have been long in use, and after all the want of lights proves nothing – does not Pliny speak & in rapturous delight of the pleasure of writing in a Room lighted by lamps.

This want of a Staircase has been brought as a proof of the building not having extended beyond its present limits – this circumstance if it proves anything – rather proves the reverse – there is no staircase or visible [probable] means of ascent to either of the

v. such a space
a room of one story [sic]
i.e. nothing over it

Is there not a proverb or expression "this work smells of the Lamp"?[16]

pyramids at Cairo which are at least nine times as high as this building would have been – it also appears from the text of Vitruvius that the Ancients thought differently of Staircases*17

In further illustration of the great variety of opinion that may be advanced respecting the steps of Staircases, we may refer to the steps, if steps they can be called, of some of the ancient temples, which are from 14 inches to two feet in height – this circumstance to those who do not look at the fact with the eyes of an Architect, might lead such persons to believe that as man in the early ages lived to prodigious ages such as 7 or 800 or even a thousand years*, so in the time of the Greeks and Romans were of such stature as to render staircases if not totally useless, at least of less importance than they are to the [degenerate (del.)] diminutive race of modern times.

* in some modern Houses produced by high genius Staircases have been entirely omitted.

* Hence the Spanish compliment [expression] "may you live 1000 years".

Those who suppose this Edifice to have been an ancient temple, reason thus: – the priests of Vesta had the care of the sacred fire and the punishment attached to neglect thereof was most examplary [sic], as well as to the Vestal Virgins who were found guilty of any in continency or human frailty*:- on this supposition, it has been imagined that the place just spoken of as a Staircase, might from its retired situation and total darkness have been the very spot where was immured & left to starve* to death in all the horrors of endless darkness there to pay the forfeit of a little human frailty:- here is food for meditation even to madness – particularly when made on the very spot where the unfortunate maiden breathed her last*.

Whilst by some this place has been looked on as a Temple, others have supposed it to have been the residence of some Magician, & in support of this opinion they speak of a large statue placed in the centre of one of the Chapels which they say might have been this very necromancer changed into marble*21

* See Historical records of them being buried alive – refer also to the painting exhibited a few years since in Spring Gardens.18

* See the Story19

Who would be a Vestal on such terms [conditions]?

*It is said the Iliad is best relished on the banks of the Scamander20

* This is not extraordinary. Lot's

for having dared to destroy the statues of the Apostles formerly placed in the niches now remaining in the in the front of this building next the park.²³ Some say his offence was not destroying the statues of the apostles but by the power of his diabolic art transforming them into statues of female[s] – there is some <u>colour</u> for this, indeed there is little doubt of the fact as several of the statues thus transformed and which correspond exactly with the dimensions of the niches are now remaining.

In support of this building having been a work of the Greeks* it is noted that in the Cavedium²⁴ there are two Caryatides or female figures supporting part of the Roof of a peristyle.²⁵ This is strong evidence* [I admit (del.)] for it is well known that the Greeks doomed to ignoble services, & also decorated their buildings with statues of, those they had taken in war* – but these statues might have been brought from Greece into this Country and here placed for ornament*

wife for looking behind her we all know was changed into a pillar of Salt & remains so to this day!²²

I judge because the transformed statues are in dimension sentate to the niches

* Surely these men do not say the disposition of the spaces remaining are any way like those of a Greek House!

* not absolutely decisive of the question altho' of this supposition

* See Vitruvius ²⁶

*Lord Elgin the modern Mummius in modern times caused various parts of antique buildings to be taken from Greece into this Country²⁷ and in the Staircase in Lansdowne House are several pieces of sculpture relative to Roman <u>Cults</u> and heathen religion.²⁸

This proves nothing. These basso rel: [ievos] might have been original Works of this Country for it is well known, an attachment to ancient customs makes us affix sculls, festoons &c.

Let us now for the present leave the further consideration of the interior and proceed to the exterior appearance of the <u>fabric</u>:- in some respects it should seem much cannot be said as to the <u>purity</u> of the Architecture of this stupendous <u>pile</u> [mass of ruin]. The principal front was probably next the great <u>Square</u> ²⁹ [area / place]* and as far as may be judged from its present state it must have been raised by some fanciful <u>mind</u> smitten with the love of novelty in <u>direct</u> [utter] defiance of all the established rules of the Architectural Schools, anxious to "Sketch a grace beyond

* now called, to indicate perhaps greatness of extent

the reach of art".³⁰ The aspect of this front being to the South, the <u>kind</u> of Eastern <u>awning</u> or <u>verandah</u> on each story [sic] is not misapplied, particularly as it does not appear to have darkened any of the Apartments or rooms of the priests\*; – had the aspect been to the North it would have altered the case, & beauty and picturesque effects must be sought for to justify the adoption of such compositions, if such adoptions can be justified or rationally accounted for – but after all if it has no better foundation – it is like beauty without and therefore not more valuable than a pudding without salt\*

\*I proceed on the idea of the place having been originally for monastic purposes.

This is a familiar expression
\* Note, on this topic much might be said, aye & usefully to[o]:– the Ancients (whom we are taught blindly to copy) did in warm climates in many of their great Temples introduce porticos & peristyles of magnificent Columns, nothing could be more appropriate in every view of the subject and consequently nothing could exceed their beauty – this fascinating and powerful arrangement the moderns have blindly followed in all situations & in all climates.

"Opened to catch cold at a Venetian door"³²

There is a striking example about the centre of the North front of this great place where an attempt has been made with two old Houses to form one great and united mass of building, and to produce this effect a grand portico is introduced, similar to those of the ancient temples with five or six tiers of windows of different forms and of unequal dimensions³³ \* [which] seem only calculated to darken the principal apartments and to increase the masons bills – this fashion of sticking on a portico of ancient Temple Architecture to a front full of small apertures if it was not very common would appear almost as preposterous as the

See Toll Houses at the entrance to the bridge at Worcester³¹

\*The architects of [concerned in] this work (for two are said to have joined their talents to produce this pasticcio of modern taste) were determined not to imitate the Bachelors dinner: tongues first cover, tongues second, tongues the third & so on.³⁴ Here we have already round & square – square & round – Oh what movement – what effects.

There is a tradition that during the progress of this [front (del.)] work much offense was taken by many to the composition of this front, doubtless from their love for pure architecture and their apprehensions lest this example might corrupt the beautiful and simple elegance of this mode then in use*, many attempts were therefore made in conjunction to render the whole abortive:- an officer yclept a district Surveyor* [36] was pushed forward [put in the front of the battle] on the occasion and boldly entered his veto against this apocryphal work – praise is however due to this dapper animal on this occasion* – he had been taught to believe that the two old women

[female statues]* in one of the fronts [of this building (del.)][38] were intended [purposely placed here] to ridicule the infantine idea in the great national work opposite[39] where two old men with Greek names on their skirts are represented embracing or rather hugging a sort of Shield*,[41] which they display to the public view, thereby to attract notice [excite curiosity] and to direct the multitude to contemplate the beauties of that great [conspicuous] Work*

ancient fashion of the Ladies, described in the Spectator as endeavouring to heighten their beauty and to increase their charms by black patches disposed in different parts of their lovely faces!!
*here show a drawing of Houses in Wimpole Street &c.[35]
* This gentleman was a great Genius, having become district surveyor he was made for the place – more of the phenomenon hereafter
* Hen. Steele . . . . bears . . . . . . [37]

* Note. Some illiberal persons have asserted that the two old Women are to represent [person-ify] the two great Architects [40] to whose combined talents we are indebted for the great display of fine Architecture opposite & who are supposed to be placed here to admire and to point out to others the beauty of that extensive pile of bricks & mortar.

* [Some have supposed (del.)] this shield has been some [sic] called 'a Guinea' – on consulting old masters I find that formerly in this country there was a piece of coin then current called a Guinea & that the [sculptures (del.)] two figures were representations of two famous misers who in this very place sold Guineas at consid-erably more than their current value, & that the whole was a sort of sign of the business carried on, in like manner as pawn brokers shops are distinguished by three great Balls & Barbers shops with long poles.   Qy. Barber Surgeons

*Note. It is curious to observe the great variety and movement in this celebrated facade – the Temple, the mansion, the humble [small (del.)] dwelling – magnifi-cence & beggary [extravagance and parsimony] are so mixed.

There are two external faces to this building. The two sides are now entirely choked up [hid] by modern buildings.⁴³

The front next the Park, as it is now commonly called, has no more pretensions to be classed with regular Architecture than the other front; this part of our building is however produced in proof of its having been a place sacred to the gods [of worship], or at least founded by some pious personages, the twelve small niches*, it may be judged from the number, were probably enriched with statues of the twelve holy Apostles*

There are no remains of these statues yet discovered but this does not weaken the probability of their having once existed. These statues were possibly made of some precious metal and removed by some daring impious violator of the most sacred rights of religion or if we suppose [supposing] them to have been made of less valuable [covetable] materials they might in that case have been destroyed by the malicious mind & puritanical zeal of infuriated fanatics* – if this place has been as now premised a place of [for] public Worship a burying place would have been attached to it, accordingly we find the ornaments with which this place is surmounted are of a kind to designate the approach to a place of sepulture, some terra santa attached to the building. This idea if established accounts for the great number of funereal decorations in this facade ⁴⁶ & scattered about the different parts of this extensive [the] building – thus pointing out by these [ornaments (del.)] decorations and monumental mementos the intention of this place in like manner as the terra santa at Pisa⁴⁷ is designated:– in later times the Legislators of the great nation [French people] have directed trees to be planted to mark out the site & to render sacred the peaceful mansions of the dead [those who sleep]:- different nations on many occasions [generally] have different methods to express [enforce] the same idea [custom]⁴⁸: – another thing to be noticed in this front is that near the present level of the ground (which by the lapse of ages must doubtless have been considerably raised)* there is a small opening or aperture which some have rashly & incon-

Front next the park
[TITLE IN MARGIN]⁴²

*See drawing No.[blank space in the text]⁴⁴
*The number does not fully determine the point. Why not of the twelve Caesars? – particularly in the circumstance of Augustus having visited this place – the Praetor being a wise man might possibly have dived into futurity and foreseeing there would be twelve Caesars provided statues and niches to place them in – in like manner as Virgil shews [sic] to _____ [blank space in the text] on his descending into the Shades, the appearances of the Augustan Lion.⁴⁵

* Note. Quote. The accounts of the statues formerly the ornaments of our Churches as at Wells etc. destroyed by the puritans:- relate the stories of the plunder of the Riches of the Church by Henry the 8th.

Note the ancients placed Columns

* Modern Rome is at least 15 feet above the level of the Ancient City⁴⁹

siderately supposed to have been for the admission of Coals into a Cellar* [50] This aperture most likely has been much narrowed by time & most probably was one of the openings or entrances leading into some of the various crypts & catacombs of which at present the remains are inconsiderable*.[51] This will account for the great number of funereal ornaments still remaining on the summit of the external wall of this front which have just been noticed [52] & which served as in other places to characterise the work:– no pillars nor fragments of pillars or burded Cypresses have been found,[53] but this deficiency of evidence may be hereafter supplied by further and deeper excavations & indeed if none of these should be found we have sufficient proofs of what here is advanced to satisfy the minds of the most sceptical.

* Note. This however has lately been almost proved to have been the fact – some person bolder than common made his way into the crypt & there, it is said, found a large quantity of Coals.
*Note. Some idle persons have supposed this hole was originally intended for the admission of coals but this is too idle a conjecture to be treated seriously – apart who brings Coals into a park – it is ridiculous & malicious.

It is difficult to determine for what purposes such a strange and mixed assemblage of ancient works or rather copies of [cast from] them, for many are not of stone or marble, have been brought together – some have supposed it might have been for the advancement of Architectural knowledge by making the young Students in that noble & useful Art who had no means of visiting Greece and Italy some better ideas of ancient Works than would be conveyed thro: the medium of drawings or prints.[55] This proposition [idea] is by far too visionary & absurd to be admitted for a moment, & yet it does appear in some degree to remove the obscurity & veil of darkness which at present envelopes the subject; at all events it is worth while to pursue the idea, circumstances may arise to justify the suggestion & to prove it less Utopian than at first view it may appear.

Let us therefore instead of supposing the building to have been a Heathen Temple to Vesta* or to some other divinity – or the palace of an Enchanter – or a Convent for Nuns – let us I say look at it merely as a dwelling, & that of an Artist, either an Architect or painter for in many respects it would be found in the arrangement of its parts to be applicable to either, the large rooms with uninterrupted light from the

On the fragments collected together in the supposed Chapel.[54]
[TITLE IN MARGIN]

*Note. It could not have been a temple to Vesta. They were always round.

North applying more particularly to the painter and the models for Architectural decoration and the extensive Library of books on that Art which are there to be seen, are circumstances indicative of the reasonableness of the latter suggestion:- to proceed – let us first enquire whether at any period any Artist of any description ever dwelt in this or in any part of these precincts? This question may be difficult of solution – we have only a choice of difficulties and the idea at least is worth pursuing: and first let us observe the imperfect motto "et filii filiorum etc." [56] indicates that not only some private person had occupied the site, but also that he had fondly flattered himself with the hope of its remaining for ages in his family – thus far we are on tenable ground but how to proceed & make the most of the point thus happily acceded by this fair construction [of] meaning of the motto. Now if it may be presumed that this individual, this identical person, was not only an Artist but an Architect – thus we through [sic] new light on the subject – let this second step be granted, do we not account most satisfactorily for that great assemblage of ancient fragments in the interior of the building which must have been placed there for the advancement and knowledge of ancient Arts & may not those varieties in the Cavedium[57] evidently the work of different artists have been fixed there in like manner to exemplify later changes in Architecture & to lay the foundation of an History of the Art itself – its origin – progress – meridian splendour & decline! – all this seems most clear & if further evidence was necessary to establish this last position of the premises having appertained to an Architect – the books on that Art attached to this day to the place would be an inescapable argument sufficient to remove all doubts in the minds of the most wary:- now in point of fact

[THE PAGE NUMBERING IN SOANE'S HAND INDICATES THAT A SINGLE LEAF NUMBERED 49–50 IS MISSING FROM THE MANUSCRIPT AT THIS POINT]

He is also recorded to have been so enthusiastically attached to his profession and so anxious to promote the knowledge of what he conceived to be its true principles that he omitted no opportunity of expressing his

See Tale of a Tub[58]

opinion on the works of all ages, not because he thought highly of his own discernment and acquired knowledge (for he was humble & modest, at the same time said to be of lively fancy) but in order to call forth the better & more useful observations of others, & thereby to provoke discussion on his favourite Art – but the man was a mere child in the World – he was indiscreet where policy is wont to impress restraint:- he had only one impression and that was what arose out of the thing spoken of – he never gave himself a moments time to reflect on who was the author of the work he criticised, he only considered whether it differed from what he conceived the laws of nature & the practice of antiquity justified & whether if the work passed without notice it might be quoted as an example & prove detrimental to what he thought good taste required & calculated to operate against improvements in Architecture:- for deviations from the principles of Ancient Architecture alas he had but too many examples in the works of his contemporaries to call forth observation – in this manner he proceeded – a friend to what he thought deserved tobe noticed, whether of true taste or of novelty, [but (del.)] a decided enemy to the affectation of it – he declared open war against such practices he considered the novelties so styled of modern work or cloaks for ignorance & whenever such examples fell in his way, however protected or sheltered by high nay even Royal Patronage, he seldom gave it much quarter – so that wherever any work was spoken of – he never considered who was the author – what his situation – or who his patrons – nor how far he had power to hurt him hereafter – he did not consider his friends – his family – his kindred – his allies and the many recruits that would enlist under him from a sense of common danger – but he went on from a pure love to promote the interests of Art, until at last he had raised a nest of wasps about him sufficient to sting the strongest man to death – Revenge <u>levelled</u> [fabricated] tales of dishonour at him, which no innocence of heart or integrity of conduct could set right and to wind up the tragedy cruelty and cowardice, twin ruffians set on by malice in the dark combined together to strike at his infirmities and mistakes:- then persecutions and other misfortunes of a more direct & domestic nature preyed on his mind – he saw the views of early youth blighted – his fairest prospects utterly destroyed – his lively character became sombre – melancholy, brooding constantly over an accumulation of evils brought him into a state little short of mental derangement, his enemies perceived this – they seized the moment – they smote his rock & he fell as many had done before him and died as was generally believed of <u>a broken heart</u>.[59]

v. quite broken hearted

From the period of his dissolution, the place has been variously occupied but always very remote from the purposes of its original formation – of course without any sentiment of respect for the place on the part of the possessor. The Gentlemen of the Law found it convenient from its vicinity to the Inns of Court – others were induced to become its occupants [for a] short time from the airiness of its situation & then, from what cause it does not exactly appear, it was supposed to be haunted, & finally in consequence of those reports it remained for ages, it may be presumed judging from its present appearance, unoccupied & unnoticed until lately its extraordinary and singular appearance claimed the attention of passers-by and produced these observations.

What an admirable lesson is this work to shew [sic] the vanity of all human expectations – the man who founded this place piously imagined that from the fruits of his honest industry & the rewards of his persistence [and] application he had laid the foundation of a family of Artists and that the filii filiorum of his loins might, smitten with the love of Art and anxious to shew their gratitude for the benefits & care & comfort they derived from it, dwell in this place from generation to generation – Alas poor man he flattered himself that a race of Artists would have been raised up whose efforts from the advantages they set out in life with – advantages the lot of the chosen few only – would have raised Architecture to its meridian splendour – Oh man, man, how short is thy foresight – in less than half a Century – in a few years – before the founder was scarcely <u>mouldered into</u> [reduced to native] dust, no

O happy Sestius
The short sum total of Life forbids us to form remote expectations
O beati Sesti
Vita summa brevis spem nos vetat inchoare longam
Horace. Ode 4, l. 15 & 16 [60]

trace remains of the Artists who were to have inhabited the place from one generation to another – & the building itself only presents a miserable picture of horrible delapidation [sic] – Oh could the dead but for a moment leave their quiet mansions – could they but even look out of their Graves and see how posterity treated them and their Works what Hell could equal their Torments.

An Antiquary

NEXT SHEET IS NUMBERED IN SOANE'S HAND AS f. 55 & 42 AND IS A VARIANT VERSION OF THE ENDING OR POSSIBLY A CANCELLED SHEET

To wind up the tragedy cruelty and Cowardice, twin ruffians set on by malice in the dark combined together to strike at his infirmities and mistakes, from these persecutions and other misfortunes of a more direct & domestic nature – his views of early youth were blighted, his fairest prospects obscured – his lively character became sombre – melancholy – brooding over will followed [sic] & it brought on a state little short of mental derangement – his enemies prevailed – they smote his rock – he fell as many had done before and died as was generally thought quite broken hearted*

From this period the place has been variously occupied – but always very remote from the purpose of its original formation – of course without any question on the part of the possessors.

What an admirable lesson does this work furnish against the vanity of human expectations – the man who founded this place piously imagined that the fruits of his honest industry & the reward of professional application [sic], he was laying the foundation of a family & that the filii filiorum of his loins should, smitten with the love of art & anxious to shew their gratitude for the benefits they thus derived from it, dwell in the place for ages [from generation to generation], that a race of artists would have been raised up whose efforts from the advantages they set out with, advantages the

*From this period the place has been occupied most strangely at one time by Gentlemen of the Law, suitable to them merely from its vicinity to the Inns of Court:- afterwards by xxx [sic]. It then, from what cause does not exactly appear, it was supposed to be haunted & finally in consequence of those reports it remained it is not known how many ages [for ages it is presumed], unoccupied, & it should seem unnoticed until its extraordinary & singular appearance claimed the attention of passers-by and produced these observations.

lot of the chosen few only, would have raised arch:[itecture] to its meridian splendour. O man, man, how short is thy foresight. In less than half a century – in a few years – before the founder was scarcely mouldering in dust, no trace to be seen of the artist within its walls, the edifice presenting only a miserable picture of frightful dilapidation – oh could the dead but leave for a moment their quiet mansions, & but look out of their graves what hell could equal their torments!

    An Antiquary

FOLLOWED BY ANOTHER ALTERNATIVE ENDING

Var:[iation]

From this period the place has been variously occupied, but always for purposes very remote from those for which it was founded & for which alone it was calculated – no wonder then that it has fallen into neglect & produces the picture represented by the annexed drawings taken in the year 1830 – compare these with representations of its original appearance. [As shewn with drawing No... Oh what a falling off – the subject becomes too gloomy to be pursued further – the pen drops from my almost paralysed hand (del.)][61]

What an admirable [exquisite] picture [a striking example] to show the vanity & mockery of all human expectations – the man who founded this place fondly imagined that the children of his children would have inhabited the place for Ages & that he had laid the foundation of an establishment which would daily gain strength and produce a race of Artists that would have done honour to their Country: – Oh what a falling off do these ruins present – the subject becomes too gloomy to be pursued – the pen drops from my almost palsied hand . . . . . . .

    v. what an impressive lesson

# Notes to the transcript

*References to works in Soane's collections are prefixed by SM for Soane Museum.*

1. The words *Crude Hints* are used by Soane to mean 'rough draft' and often appear in the titles of early drafts of his Royal Academy lectures.

2. At the time he was writing *Crude Hints* Soane was in the process of building No. 13 on the 'ruins' of the earlier house on the site which he had demolished. Soane's new construction site was 'in some degree attached' to his existing Museum at the rear of No. 12 Lincoln's Inn Fields.

3. This is a tongue in cheek reference to that fact that Soane was at this date in his third phase of building work. In 1792-4 he had demolished and rebuilt No. 12 Lincoln's Inn Fields. In 1807 he purchased No. 13, next door, and in 1808-9 he had demolished the stable block at the back and constructed a 'gallery for plaster casts' and a new office.

4. Soane had demolished the previous houses on both the No. 12 and the No. 13 site to construct his buildings.

5. In using a votive foot and hand as his first clue to the origin of the building Soane may be remembering the impressive fragments of a colossal statue of Constantine the Great, including a head, hand and foot, in the courtyard of the Palazzo dei Conservatori on the Capitoline Hill in Rome which he would have seen in 1778-9 on his Grand Tour.

6. This is a reference to a book so far unidentified. The closest item in Soane's Library is Le Fevre De Morsan, *Manners and Customs of the Romans* 1740 (SM GL1B).

7. This is a reference to ammonite fossils, the origin of the name lying in their resemblance to the curly rams' or goats' horns which are the attribute of Jupiter Ammon – a reference to the legend of his birth in a cave on Crete after which he was brought up by Nymphs on the slopes of Mount Ida and suckled by the goat Amalthea. The earliest inventories of Soane's collection (1837) list three such large ammonites, displayed on the skyline of the rear buildings of the Museum and these were probably already in Soane's collection in 1812. Soane's 1802 description of his mock-ruins at Pitzhanger mentions a 'horn of Ammon' and it is possible that reference is also to an ammonite fossil.

8. Soane may have had in mind the Ionic columns he was planning to install round the central Monument Court at No. 13 (two were finally installed but early sketches of *c.* July–August 1812, SM 32/3/28 and SM 32/3/32 show that he initially envisaged more). Alternatively Soane may be thinking of the Ionic colonnade he envisaged on the front of his grandiose scheme for Nos 13-15

Lincoln's Inn Fields, drawn up in January 1813 but probably in his mind at the time *Crude Hints* was written (see Fig. 1).

9. The Sphinx, Griffon and lamb carried Soane back to the mysteries of Egypt (in lecture XI he referred to the sphinx as 'emblematical of the mysteries of the Egyptian theology'), Rome and both Jewish and Christian symbolism.

10. The wine cellar beneath Soane's office at the back of No. 13 probably inspired this reference to a 'great crypt'. The cellar was extensive with its flat ceiling supported by fluted columns.  Several drawings of 1808-9 envisage it as a crypt or catacomb with ruinous columns and dank atmosphere, filled with objects including not only fragments and casts but also the wooden Egyptian mummy case still in Soane's collection (see Fig. 9).  The wine cellar was, however, not part of the museum's display area until 1834-5 when it was finally converted into the 'Egyptian Crypt'.

11. The ancient Mesopotamian city of Nineveh (Kuyunjik), the ruins of which lie in modern Iraq, was one of the great cities of the Assyrian kingdom.  In Soane's day it was known only from Roman and Greek writings – the Assyrian and Babylonian cuneiform script was not deciphered until later in the 19th century.  The ruins of Nineveh were not rediscovered and excavated until the 1840s, after Soane's death. Soane is referring here to the Old Testament, Book of Jonah, Chapter 3, verse 3: *So Jonah arose, and went to Nineveh, according to the word of the LORD. Now Nineveh was an exceeding great city of three days' journey*. The usual interpretation of this is that the writer was referring to the circuit of Nineveh, and meant that the city was so large that it would take a man three days to go round it, walking at a normal pace.

12. Thomas Sandby when Professor of Architecture at the Royal Academy, reminded his students at the start of his 1st lecture that *The first piece of architecture that we read of is the Ark of Noah* (MS copy of Sandby's lectures SM AL 31B).  Soane attended Sandby's lectures when a student and later stated in his own 1st lecture (as delivered in 1817) that Noah's Ark *contained on each floor upwards of 30,000 superficial feet, more than any ship in the British navy* (SM AL Soane Case 155, Lectures of Architecture, Royal Academy, f.48) and illustrated this point with a drawing comparing the Ark with a modern man o' war (Fig. 10).

13. In this paragraph and the attached note Soane imagines the visitor finding the inscription 'Mihi turpe relinqui est' ('it would be disgraceful if I fell behind') among the ruins.  In the first reference to the existence of a single founder or builder of the ruins the visitor is asked to imagine this founder 'recollecting' his own use of the quotation when in Rome and 'deliberating between going and staying'.  This is a reference to the moment in early 1780 when Soane was in Rome and had to decide whether or not to give up the final third year of his Grand Tour in order to return home and take up the offer of work from the Frederick Hervey, Bishop of Derry, at Downhill in

*Fig. 9 Sectional perspective design for the Museum at the rear of the house drawn by James Adams on 25 June 1808 and showing the atmospheric contrast Soane envisaged between his ground-floor Museum and the basement Crypt or Catacombs below (SM Vol. 83/37)*

*Fig. 10  Soane Royal Academy Lecture drawing comparing Noah's Ark with a modern man-o-war ship (SM 23/2/10)*

Ireland. Soane decided to return but the offer of work did not materialise and after six weeks in Ireland he returned to London somewhat chastened and embittered to set up his own practice.

In the note to this paragraph Soane speculates that the inscription is a fragment of an Ode to the Roman Emperor Augustus. In fact it is a quote from Horace, *Ars Poetica* (line 417), a poem written in about 19 BC advising poets on the art of writing poetry and drama, and is Horace's ironical comment concerning the need for genius to be sustained by experience. This Latin phrase obviously meant a lot to Soane. He may first have come across it as a pupil in the office of George Dance – it was the motto inscribed on Dance's prize-winning 'Magnifica Galleria' design for the Ducal Academy of Parma in 1763. The motto was used as a means of identification at Parma for the otherwise anonymous competitors. Soane displayed copies of Dance's Parma drawings at his own Royal Academy lectures. A proposal (not used) for the title page of Soane's first book *Designs in Architecture* (1778) incorporates the same motto. A plan of his original design for the Infirmary at the Royal Hospital, Chelsea (SM 67/5/24) drawn in August 1809 is inscribed *to the Lords and other Commissioners for managing the affairs of Chelsea Hospital MIHI TURPE RELINQUI EST* and the motto also appears in the Royal Academy exhibition catalogue 1826 (No. 869) in connection with his scheme for the completion of the Board of Trade and Downing Street.

It also appears on the title page of his publication, *Designs for Public and Private Buildings,* 1828 (see Robin Middleton, 'The History of John Soane's "Designs for Public and Private Buildings"', *The Burlington Magazine,* August 1996).

14. Sammu-Ramat, more famously known as Semiramis, is a legendary figure who was Queen of Assyria in the 8th century BC. Soane's comments may in part reflect the reference in *De Dea Syria* by Lucian (writing in the second century AD) to her having constructed 'many monuments of grandeur and magnificence': he says she is reputed by some to have built the temple of Aphrodite in Libanus. The Greek historian Herodotus ascribes to her the construction of the embankments around Babylon to control the River Euphrates. It seems that the name of Semiramis came to be applied to various monuments in Western Asia and Asia Minor, the origin of which was forgotten or unknown.

15. This is a rare reference to Piranesi in Soane's writings. The word 'Carcerian' is in reference to Piranesi's famous etchings of *capricci* of imaginary prisons, the *Carceri*. Soane owned a copy of the second issue (1753-54) of the first edition *Invenzioni Capric di Carceri…*, published in 1750 (SM AL7C). Soane speculates that because the staircase void is windowless (there are a number of windows above ground-floor level but the structure was only partly built at the time of writing) it cannot be a staircase but could be a prison. Soane's own preference for top-lit spaces is expressed not just in the staircase at Lincoln's Inn Fields but in the elaborate roofscape of the 'Museum' at the back of the site, with its double-height tribune, the 'Dome Area' at its heart.

16. This may be a paraphrase of a comment in Laurence Sterne's Dedication at the beginning of his novel *Tristram Shandy* in which he says *I should have no objection to this method, but that I think it must smell too strong of the lamp.*

17. The *De architectura* by Vitruvius Pollio (*c*.90–*c*.20 BC) is the only complete treatise on architecture to survive from antiquity. Soane seems to be referring here to Book IX, Chapter II, in which Vitruvius discusses how to calculate the heights of steps using Pythagorean principles to create an even series of right-angled triangles.

18. The Vestal Virgins were chosen from patrician Roman families by the *pontifex maximus* to watch in turn by day and night the fire in the temple of Vesta in the Forum at Rome and have custody of its sacred objects. Their purity was all-important and any Vestal found guilty of unchastity was entombed alive. The Younger Pliny in his *Letters*, Book IV, letter XI describes an instance under the Emperor Domitian when the vestal Cornelia Maximilla was buried alive in a subterranean cavern.

The Society of Artists of Great Britain held their annual exhibitions at the Great Room in Spring Gardens near Charing Cross from 1761 to 1777 and in 1780. In 1767 George Willison exhibited as no. 181 a *Portrait of a young lady in the character of a Vestal* and it may be this painting that Soane is recalling here (see Algernon Graves: *The Society of Artists of Great Britain ... The Free Society of Artists...A complete Dictionary of Contributors ....*, 1907).

19. Pliny, *Letters*, Book IV, letter XI, op. cit.

20. The River Scamander was in the region of Troas, close to the City of Ilium (Troy), the subject of much of Homer's epic. In *Iliad* XXII (149 ff.), Homer states that the river had two springs: one produced warm water; the other yielded cold water, regardless of the season.

21. Soane must have in mind here the cast of the Apollo Belvedere which dominates his Museum. This had been made in Rome for the Richard Boyle, 3rd Earl of Burlington and was presented to Soane by the architect John White. It arrived at Lincoln's Inn Fields in November 1811 – Soane had to demolish part of the rear elevation to put it into position. The speculation that it might be in one of a series of 'Chapels' is interesting as the Dome Area, where it was in reality placed, is surrounded by arches and filled with what could be regarded as 'memorials', ancient and modern, in a somewhat chapel-like manner. It also, of course, has a funereal basement beneath like the crypt beneath a chapel. It is fascinating that the idea of the house as a 'series of chapels' appears here at

*Fig. 11 Design for the rear façade of Nos 12 & 13 Lincoln's Inn Fields, c. July-August 1812 (SM 32/3/43)*

such an early stage of the development of Soane's Museum – over the next 25 years he developed interiors at No. 13 which can be interpreted as a series of 'shrines'. See Helen Dorey 'Death and Memory: the Architecture of Legacy in Sir John Soane's Museum' in *Death and Memory*, Sir John Soane's Museum/Pimpernel Press, 2015. See also Fig. 14.

22. The story is told in the Old Testament, Book of Genesis, Chapter 19.

23. The 'Front next the Park' is the rear façade of Nos 12 & 13 on to Whetstone Park, or *Weston's Park* as it was during Soane's lifetime. This façade incorporates a row of blind niches (see Fig. 11) which were never intended to house statues in reality.

24. A Cavaedium is defined in *Nicholson's Architectural Dictionary*, 1819 (SM AL41B) as 'from the Latin *cava* and *aedium*, a vacant space within the body of a building; in a Roman house it was what we now call a court'. Soane is probably thinking of his 'Monument Court', under construction at the time (see Fig. 12).

25. The statement that caryatids supporting a peristyle indicate that the building is a work of the Greeks is a reference to the celebrated caryatid porch of the Erechtheion on the Acropolis in Athens.

Soane's reference to caryatids in the *cavedium* [sic] probably refers to the two female term figures set into the north wall of the Monument Court during construction in summer 1812 (Museum nos MC31 and MC33; shown in Fig. 12). There is a third term figure (Museum no. MC28) which Soane refers to as a caryatid in his *Description* of 1835, but it was probably installed in the courtyard after 1812 and seems unlikely to be referred to here.

In 2014, during the restoration of framed works from the North Drawing Room a large number of 'waste' drawings were discovered, pasted together to form the backings to a number of framed works. From the back of SM P275 a hitherto unknown design for the façade of No. 13 Lincoln's Inn Fields emerged, dated *July 27th 1812* in which a series of caryatids are shown holding up a porch-like feature at the top of the façade in a proposal much closer to a recreation of the porch of the Erechtheion in Athens than what was eventually executed (Fig. 13). In the back of drawing SM P282 another complete drawing, a detail of a similar design for the top of the façade dated *July 24th 1812*, was found.

26. In Book 1, chapter 1 of *De architectura*, in describing the origins of caryatides (literal meaning: 'maidens of Caryæ') Vitruvius explains that the city of Carya [Karyæ] joined the Persians in a War against the Greeks. The Greeks took the City, carried its women into slavery and to perpetuate the memory of their triumph and to ensure that the crime of the Caryans in taking up arms against them was never forgotten, created female figures shown draped and suffering under the burden with which they were loaded.

*Fig. 12 Monument Court under construction drawn by George Basevi (1794-1845), a pupil of John Soane, 31 August–2 September 1812 (SM Vol. 83/5)*

27. Lucius Mummius Achaicus was Consul in 146 BC and became Roman commander in the war against the Achaean Confederacy in that year. He was responsible for the sack of Corinth after which its art treasures were shipped to Italy. Soane refers to this episode in his second Royal Academy lecture recounting that the Romans were only interested in conquest and plunder and Mummius had such lack of understanding of art that when he sent the spoils of Corinth to Rome *he threatened those who had the care of the pictures and statues that if any were lost or purloined they should produce him others.*

Thomas Bruce 7th Earl of Elgin (1766-1841) was appointed Ambassador to the Sublime Porte at Constantinople in 1799. He set out to study the monuments of Athens, then within the Turkish dominions, employing a team of artists there from 1800. From 1801 he had a *firman* (licence) from the Porte permitting him not only to fix scaffolding round the Parthenon in order to and take casts in plaster and gypsum but also to take away *any piece of stone with old inscriptions or figures.* Shipments began in 1801 and the majority of the Elgin collection of marbles arrived in England in 1804. After Elgin himself left Turkey in 1803 his artist in charge, Lusieri, continued to direct excavations in Greece and as late as 1811-1812 the last consignment of 80 cases of antiquities arrived in London. Soane's comparison of Elgin with Mummius seems to reflect the outcry that there was about Elgin's conduct over the removal of antiquities. The propriety of his actions was questioned and he was accused of vandalism, rapacity and dishonesty. This criticism found its most extreme expression in Byron's *Curse of Minerva* (written in Athens in March 1807). The criticism spurred Elgin to open his collection to the public, from 1807 in a makeshift museum at his own house in Park Lane and later at Burlington House in Piccadilly. Soane was writing *Crude Hints* the year after Elgin first offered his marbles to the nation in 1811 for £62,440. Once the Elgin marbles were on public display critics accepted the supreme merits of the Parthenon sculptures and eventually a Select Committee was appointed in 1816 to look into acquiring them for the nation. On its recommendation they were purchased for £35,000.

Soane's own view of Elgin probably altered with general critical opinion. David Watkin quotes a later instance of Soane noting in preparation for a lecture *When speaking of the number of statues in Rome, quote how they became possessed of them, not from Roman talent, nor even love of art. The objects were invaluable intrinsically which at first executed the cupidity and afterwards gave the Romans a taste for those arts. In this view how much praise is due to Lord Elgin.* (SM AL Soane Case 177, fol. 87 quoted in David Watkin, *Soane Enlightenment Thought and the Royal Academy Lectures*, 1996).

28. Lansdowne House in Berkeley Square was begun by the architect Robert Adam in 1762 for the 3rd Earl of Bute who sold it unfinished to the 1st Marquis of Lansdowne (1737-1805) better known as Lord Shelburne. The house was completed in 1768 apart from the Gallery which was subsequently fitted up as a Library by George Dance junior in 1788-91. The Marquis' Gallery of antiquities, purchased from the well-known artist and dealer in antiquities, Gavin Hamilton, was well known and had been offered for sale in 1810, two years before the writing of *Crude Hints*.

*Fig. 13 Unexecuted design for the façade of 13 Lincoln's Inn Fields, dated July 27th 1812, discovered in the back of a framed work at the Museum in 2014 (SM P275.viii)*

*Fig. 14 Sectional perspective of the Dome Area and Breakfast Room at 13 Lincoln's Inn Fields looking east drawn in 1818 by Soane's pupil Frank Copland (it is incorrectly dated 1817 in a later hand). This shows the figure of Apollo as originally placed by Soane on the east side of the dome (SM Vol. 83/1)*

29. Lincoln's Inn Fields.

30. This is a misquote from Alexander Pope's *An Essay of Criticism* (1711): *Great wits may sometimes gloriously offend / And rise to faults true critics dare not mend. / From vulgar bounds with brave disorder part / And snatch a grace beyond the reach of art.* The *European Magazine*, November 1812, refers to the fact that Thomas Sandby used the last line of this quotation annually in his lectures although it does not appear in Soane's MS copy (op. cit. note 12).

31. Worcester Bridge and its approaches was designed by John Gwynn (1713-86) in 1771-80 and opened in 1781. Gwynn was a founder member of the Royal Academy and exhibited there from 1769-72. In 1770 he exhibited *A plan, elevation and section of the bridge to be built over the Severn at Worcester*. In Soane's library there is a copy of *A Concise History of Worcester* 1808 (SM AL32D) which includes a plan showing the bridge with the toll houses at the west end. There are no drawings of the bridge in the Soane collection.

32. This is a misquote of a passage in Alexander Pope's 'Epistle to Richard Boyle, Earl of Burlington on the Use of Riches' in *Moral Essays* (published December 1731) in which the poet refers to those who misapply the elements of classical architecture as *imitating fools* who use triumphal arches for garden gates, apply the classical orders to patched up walls and *call the winds through long arcades to roar / Proud to catch cold at a Venetian door*. David Watkin (op. cit) notes that Soane read Pope frequently, making extensive notes from his *Moral Essays* and *Essay on Criticism* and that these were quoted frequently in his Royal Academy lectures. It is interesting to note that Thomas Sandby used the same quotation in his Lecture 1, commenting on the absurdity of English architects using designs suitable only for southern climates and adding that *Pope, we may remember tells us of those who are 'Proud to catch cold at a Venetian door' and ridicules, in most pointed Satire, the false taste of such as transplant Italian Architecture into England.*

33. This reference to an attempt to create one unified building *about the centre of the North front* of Lincoln's Inn Fields seems to anticipate Soane's own design for a unified triple façade for Nos 13-15 which he was working on in January 1813 (see Fig. 1). The marginal note alongside refers to two architects having been said to have joined their talents to produce this pasticcio of modern taste – was Soane perhaps thinking of Joseph Michael Gandy who drew up the proposal or was he confusing this section with the section referring to the Royal College of Surgeons in which he mentions that two architects were involved?

34. Soane's reference to a Bachelor's Dinner is a complex dining analogy comparing a tedious and boring building with a bachelor's dinner consisting only of tongue. The origin of Soane's use of the term 'a Batchelor's Dinner' as meaning a monotonous meal may lie in Jonathan Swift's *Polite Conversation* (1738), Dialogue 1, in which Batchelor's fare was defined as *bread and cheese and*

*kisses*. This definition of Bachelor's fare appears in *A Classical Dictionary of the Vulgar Tongue*, 1796, a copy of which is in Soane's library (SM GL BR1C). It was also used as the title for a number of popular prints and ballads in the late 18th and early 19th centuries.

35. The use of the word 'show' in this note seems to imply that Soane is contemplating using an illustration of houses in Wimpole Street to accompany this text as a lecture or as a publication. The antiquarian flavour of the text makes it difficult to be clear about which was intended by the use of the word 'show' but references to illustrations also appear elsewhere in the text. There are no drawings of houses in Wimpole Street in Soane's collection nor are houses in Wimpole Street singled out for praise in Soane's lectures. However, Soane seems to be citing them here as a praiseworthy example of archetypal Georgian symmetry.

36. The district surveyor referred to is William Kinnard (*c*.1788-1839), District Surveyor for St Giles-in-the-Fields and St George's Bloomsbury since 1807 (see Colvin, *A Biographical Dictionary of British Architects 1600-1840, 3rd edition, Yale University Press, 1995*). Soane is being self-consciously archaic by using *yclept* instead of the more modern 'called'.

37. It has not been possible to decipher this marginal note which seems to begin with the name Henry Steele. No-one of this name is listed in Colvin (op. cit.) or the *Dictionary of National Biography* and the name does not appear amongst Soane's neighbours and contacts or amongst the lawyers or journalists connected with the façade dispute or as the author of any book or pamphlet in his library. There was a printer of this name with premises near the Bank of England in the 1770s but there is no known connection with Soane.

38. The 'two old women' referred to are the two Coade Stone caryatids on the façade of Soane's Museum. These appear on the design drawings for the front façade of July and August 1812 (see Fig. 6) although at the time Soane was writing *Crude Hints* they were not yet in place. In Soane's progress notebook for the building work he recorded on October 3rd 1812 *The two statues were brought here this morning punctually to Mr. Scoly's promise between 10 and 11 and in the course of the afternoon they were raised into their proper places and the workmen began to remove the upper part of the scaffolding* (SM Archive 7/A/8).

39. The Royal College of Surgeons (begun in 1806 but not completed until 1813; see Fig. 4).

40. George Dance the younger (1741-1825) and James Lewis (*c*.1751-1820). Soane entered Dance's office at the age of 15 and in later life referred to him as his 'revered' master. He was much influenced by his work and despite the falling-out between them as a result of the Royal Academy lecture dispute following Soane's criticism of the Royal College of Surgeons building (along with Smirke's Covent Garden Theatre: see Introduction, p. 5) was, for most of his life, in close personal

touch with Dance. He purchased Dance's drawings in the 'Dance Cabinet' after his death, adding a black base decorated with pineapples as symbols of eternity and hanging the cabinet with his own drawings in a subtle tribute from pupil to master.

41. The statues represent Machaon and Podalirius, the surgeon sons of Aesculapius, holding a cartouche bearing the College arms (carved by Rossi in 1811).

Soane's 1830, 1832 and 1835 *Descriptions* of his residence all refer to the fact that the caryatids on No. 13 are *nearly opposite those of Machaon and Podalirius in the front of the College of Surgeons, on the South side of the square.*

Soane's digression (in the right-hand column) on the subject of the two statues perhaps holding a 'guinea' in reference to two misers who sold Guineas at more than their value 'in this very place' is mysterious and it has not been possible to identify a pawnbroker in Lincoln's Inn Fields. The gold guinea coin was first struck after the re-coinage of 1696. The last guinea coin was struck in 1813. The supply of gold was a particular problem at the end of the 18th century following the various revolutionary wars and upheavals.

42. Whetstone Park façade i.e. rear façade.

43. A reference to the fact that No. 13 is in the centre of a terrace.

44. Soane probably had in mind drawing SM 32/3/43 (see Fig. 11). His niches are far too shallow to take statues so this section of *Crude Hints* is purely speculative.

45. This is a reference to the passage in Book VI of Virgil's *Aeneid* in which the Trojan hero Aeneas descends to the underworld to meet his dead father Anchises. Anchises reveals to Aeneas his future destiny. He shows him the future rulers of Rome, his descendants, awaiting rebirth and names each one. The term 'Augustan Lion' is used here to mean 'the Roman emperors'.

46. This is a reference to the carved blocks flanking the central section of the rear façade, on the coping (see Fig. 11). These are based on the lids of Antique cinerary urns of which there are numerous examples in the Soane collection. Soane used similar segmental pediments adorned with beribboned wreaths on various of his tomb designs.

47. The Campo Santo in Pisa is a vast 13th-century cloister containing numerous Roman sarcophagi and other fragments. Many 18th-century theorists envisaged the ideal cemetery as a cloister similar to the Campo Santo. Soane was immensely impressed by it and had a large drawing of it prepared for use in his Royal Academy lectures (SM 76/7/5).

48. This is perhaps a reference to the enlightenment ideals of 18th-century France. Rousseau was buried on a tree covered island at Ermenonville (a sketch of which, in Soane's hand, is in his copy

of Rousseau's *Confessions*) and the theorist Quatremère de Quincy envisaged the ideal cemetery as being a cloister like the Campo Santo in Pisa but planted with cypresses and yews to create an atmosphere of 'sacred melancholy'.

The section of text could also be read as implying that Napoleon's government (after taking over Pisa after his invasion of Italy in 1797) decreed that the central garden within the Campo Santo in Pisa be laid out with trees: this does not seem to be the case.

49. As a consequence of this Soane, like all other Grand Tourists before him, saw many of the most celebrated temples in the Roman Forum in a partially buried state. It was only later in the 19th century that the Forum was excavated to the level of the paving of the ancient city.

50. In a design drawing for Soane's Museum building across the back of No. 13 dated *July 28th 1808* (SM 32/3/48) a *coal cellar* is shown occupying the rear basement of No. 12, Soane's existing house. This coal cellar does not appear on other drawings but may well have existed and be what Soane is thinking of with this reference. It is interesting that on the same design drawing an aperture is envisaged on the north side of Soane's new wine cellar, in the basement beneath his office, *For letting / down Pipes / of wine*, so he was intending to install some sort of trap door or opening in the ground floor to allow wine delivered to the Office door in Whetstone Park to be lowered into the cellar.

51. The idea of crypts and catacombs below the Museum is one which appears on drawings for the basement of the 'Museum' at the back of No. 13 from the earliest design drawings in 1808. As built the area beneath the main dome skylight was treated like a catacomb, with fragments scattered on the floor within the arches – which almost appear semi-excavated coming straight out of the ground (see Fig. 15). After 1824, with the arrival of the sarcophagus of Seti I this area was referred to as the 'Sepulchral Chamber'. Soane took the idea further even later in life with the construction of a further small area actually called the 'Catacombs and Champs Elysées' in 1825 (constructed like Roman *columbaria*) and the creation of his 'Egyptian Crypt' in the mid-1830s.

52. Another reference to the carved stones on top of the rear façade.

53. Soane is probably here thinking not just of 18th-century French thinking (see note 48) but also of the tradition that Roman Imperial mausolea (such as those of Augustus and Hadrian) incorporated cypress groves. He seems to be being consciously archaic in using the term 'burded': burd is a Middle English word of obscure origin meaning 'bird'. Soane was also aware that the Romans believed that their ancestors had buried their dead inside their town houses. An early design plan for the basement of Soane's Museum at the back of No. 13, dated *July 28th 1808* denotes the basement as *catacombs* and shows a *mausoleum* extending into the central courtyard (SM 32/3/48).

*Fig. 15 Joseph Michael Gandy, view of the 'Dome' of John Soane's Museum, looking east, 1811 (SM P384)*

*Fig. 16 Joseph Michael Gandy, View of the 'Dome' of Sir John Soane's Museum by night, looking south-east, showing Soane on the right gesturing to his collections, 1811 (SM 14/6/4)*

*Fig. 17 Joseph Michael Gandy, Architectural Ruins – a Vision, 1798, showing the Rotunda of Soane's Bank of England as a ruin. This imaginary view was drawn in the year the Rotunda was completed but not exhibited at the Royal Academy until many years later, in 1832 (SM P127)*

*Fig. 18 Joseph Michael Gandy, A Bird's-eye View of the Bank of England, 1830 (SM P267)*

54. The *supposed chapel* is Soane's double-height tribune or 'dome' at the back of No. 13 (see Figs 14 and 15). See also note 21.

55. This passage illuminates Soane's motives for setting up his Museum. Soane was well aware that many of his Royal Academy students would never see Rome, closed to them as a result of the Napoleonic wars.

56. This is the second inscription (here called a *motto*) supposedly discovered in the ruins. Like the first one it is fragmentary, *et filii filiorum* ('and the sons of his sons....'). There is a Latin inscription containing this phrase *ET FILII FILIORUM ET SEMEN ILLORUM HABITABUNT IN SAECULA* set into the façade of the fine Renaissance Palazzo Canossa in Verona designed by Sanmichele, a building Soane must have seen and admired. He acquired a measured drawing of it by Gaetano Avesani almost certainly at the time of his visit as it seems to be dated (from the watermark) 1779 when Soane was in Italy (SM 44/10/2).

57. Cavedienne = Cavedium (see note 24). The walls of Soane's Monument Court were set with examples of the work of different centuries deliberately placed there, as Soane put it later in his 1835 *Description* as *an assemblage of ancient and modern Art* to exemplify the history of architecture. This idea was amplified in 1819 with the installation of the *pasticcio* – a 30ft column of fragments symbolising architecture, in the centre of the yard.

58. Jonathan Swift (1667-1745) *The Tale of a Tub* (1704). This satirical work is a general denunciation of shams and pedantry, especially ridiculing theological pedantry. There is a copy of the Works of Jonathan Swift in 25 volumes in Soane's Library (SM GL17.C.D.E).

59. The whole of the preceding section of text refers to the Royal Academy lecture dispute and its effect on Soane.

60. Soane's library contains three translations of the works of Horace (65-8 BC) in English and two in French. This quotation is from *Odes* Book I, iv and refers to Lucius Sestius, consul in 23 BC, the year that the *Odes* appeared.

61. In this variant ending Soane projects forward in time to visualise the Museum as it might be depicted in 1830, in ruins, and asks the onlooker to compare these with representations of its original appearance *as shewn with drawing No.....* The drawings of its original appearance Soane was thinking of at the time he was writing *Crude Hints* would have included Figs 15 and 16. Soane never did have his Museum depicted as if in ruins but earlier he had commissioned from Gandy an imaginary view of the Rotunda and the Dividend Warrant Offices at the Bank of England in ruins, entitled *Architectural Ruins – a Vision*, drawn in the year of its completion (1798) but not exhibited at the Royal Academy until 1832 (Fig. 17). Many years later he commissioned a bird's-eye cutaway

perspective of the Bank of England by Gandy, exhibited in the year 1830, which shows the Bank as a poetic ruinscape, the ground falling away dramatically as if not just the Bank but the earth itself beneath the City of London is collapsing (Fig. 18). Bizarrely, Soane's vision of the future ruin of his Bank came to pass in the late 1920s when his great banking halls were demolished when the interiors at the Bank were rebuilt (Fig. 19) – an appropriate postscript, just over a century later, to the fevered imaginings of 1812 of which *Crude Hints* is the expression.

*Fig. 19 Photograph from* The Times, *1 May 1925, showing the Rotunda at Soane's Bank of England during its demolition*